Brilliant Activities for

Reading Comprehension, Year 1

Engaging Stories and Activities to Develop Comprehension Skills

Charlotte Makhlouf

Brilliant
PUBLICATIONS

Brilliant Publications publishes many other practical resource books for primary school teachers, a few of which are listed below. You may find more details on our website: www.brilliantpublications.co.uk.

Brilliant Activities for Reading Comprehension Series

Other publications

Published by Brilliant Publications
Unit 10
Sparrow Hall Farm
Edlesborough
Dunstable
Bedfordshire
LU6 2ES, UK

Tel: 01525 222292

E-mail: info@brilliantpublications.co.uk

Website: www.brilliantpublications.co.uk

The name Brilliant Publications and the logo are registered trademarks.

Written by Charlotte Makhlouf

Illustrated by Calvin Innes, Pat Murray and Frank Endersby

Cover illustration by Calvin Innes

Front cover designed by Brilliant Publications

© Text: Charlotte Mahklouf 2012

© Design: Brilliant Publications 2012

ISBN: 978-0-85747-482-7

e-book ISBN: 978-0-85747-489-6

First printed and published in the UK in 2012

The right of Charlotte Makhlouf to be identified as the author of this work has been asserted by herself in accordance with the Copyright, Designs and Patents Act 1988.

Contents

Introduction

The importance of reading for meaning should never be underestimated. Whilst many young children might be able to decode quite complex texts, it is vital that they understand what they read. More importantly, it is fundamental that they enjoy what they are reading.

Over my 15 years of experience, I have used a number of comprehension books as part of my English teaching. Very few of them have engaged the children who are being asked to read and understand them. I decided that if we are asking children to read, understand and answer questions from a passage, that passage should at least engage their attention, and indeed their teacher's attention as well.

The passages in the **Brilliant Activities for Reading Comprehension Series** are designed to give children valuable reading practice through varied, enjoyable texts. The passages begin in the **Year 1** book with simple picture comprehension. They gradually increase in difficulty as you progress through the book, and through the series, encouraging pupils to use a range of decoding strategies and to develop their ability to read for meaning. The passages in this series are entirely fictional and it s hoped that both teachers and pupils will find them humorous.

Teachers should read the texts (or, in the case of this book, look at the pictures) with the children and discuss them thoroughly before allowing them to proceed to the activities. If you are using the e-book version, you can display the pages on the interactive white board.

In the **Year 1** book there are first a series of True/False questions and then a range of questions that require a full sentence as a response. The Extension work sections require more open-ended questions enabling the pupils to provide a more personal response. Space has been provided for them to answer on the page, but you could ask them to write the answers in their workbooks. Answers are provided on pages 108–113. On pages 7–11 there are some suggestions for ways in which the children can follow up this work in other areas of the curriculum, thus providing a cross-curricular aspect. These activities are ideal for children who finish quickly.

The **Brilliant Activities for Reading Comprehension Series** provides the teacher with a basis for ensuring progression. The activities give pupils:

◆   the ability to select or retrieve information in order to answer the questions successfully using a full sentence

◆   the opportunity to deduce, infer or interpret information, events or ideas from the texts

◆   the opportunity to identify and comment on the structure and organization of the text and comment on the writer's use of language at word and sentence level

◆   the chance to comment on cultural, social or historical traditions and the impact the text may have on the reader.

The **Brilliant Activities for Reading Comprehension Series** provides an invaluable resource for assessing pupil progress in reading. The key assessment criteria from the National Strategies for levels 1 and 2 for reading are listed, for your convenience, on pages 5–6.

Assessing Pupil Progress

The activities in this book will help to assess the following criteria:

AF1 – use a range of strategies, including accurate decoding of text, to read for meaning

Level 1 **In some reading, usually with support:**
- ◆ some high frequency and familiar words read fluently and automatically
- ◆ decode familiar and some unfamiliar words using blending as the prime approach
- ◆ some awareness of punctuation.

Level 2 **In some reading:**
- ◆ range of key words read on sight
- ◆ unfamiliar words decoded using appropriate strategies, eg blending sounds
- ◆ some fluency and expression, eg taking account of punctuation, speech marks.

AF2 – understand, describe, select or retrieve information, events or ideas from texts and use quotation and reference to text

Level 1 **In some reading, usually with support:**
- ◆ some simple points from familiar texts recalled
- ◆ some pages/sections of interest located, eg favourite characters/events/information/pictures.

Level 2 **In some reading:**
- ◆ some specific, straightforward information recalled, eg names of characters, main ingredients
- ◆ generally clear idea of where to look for information, eg about characters, topics.

AF3 – deduce, infer or interpret information events or ideas from text

Level 1 **In some reading, usually with support:**
- ◆ reasonable inference at a basic level, eg identifying who is speaking in a story
- ◆ comments/questions about meaning of parts of text, eg details of illustrations diagrams, changes in font style.

Level 2 **In some reading:**
- ◆ simple, plausible inference about events and information, using evidence from text, eg how a character is feeling, what makes a plant grow
- ◆ comments based on textual clues sometimes misunderstood.

AF4 – identify and comment on the structure and organization of texts, including grammatical and presentational features at text level

Level 1 **In some reading, usually with support:**
- ◆ some awareness of meaning of simple text features, eg font style, labels, titles.

Level 2   In some reading:
- ◆ some awareness of use of features of organization, eg beginning and ending of story, types of punctuation.

AF5 – explain and comment on writer's use of language, including grammatical and literary features at word and sentence level

Level 1   In some reading, usually with support:
- ◆ comments on obvious features of language, eg rhymes and refrains, significant words and phrases.

Level 2   In some reading:
- ◆ some effective language choices noted, eg '"slimy" is a good word there'
- ◆ some familiar patterns of language identified, eg once upon a time, first, next, last.

AF6 – identify and comment on writer's purposes and viewpoints, and the overall effect of the text on the reader

Level 1   In some reading, usually with support:
- ◆ some simple comments about preferences, mostly linked to own experience.

Level 2   In some reading:
- ◆ some awareness that writers have viewpoints and purposes, eg 'it tells you how to do something', 'she thinks it's not fair'
- ◆ simple statements about likes and dislikes in reading, sometimes with reasons.

AF7 – relate texts to their social, cultural and historical traditions

Level 1   In some reading, usually with support:
- ◆ a few basic features of well-known story and information texts distinguished, eg what typically happens to good and bad characters, differences between type of text in which photographs or drawings are used.

Level 2   In some reading:
- ◆ general features of a few text types identified.

Cross-curricular Activities

Animals page 12

- Draw a picture of animals doing funny things.
- Make a collar for a dog out of junk materials.
- Make up a short play in which animals talk together.
- Choose any animal. Find out about its habitat then draw where it lives.
- Make up number stories about the fish that Tortoise catches. For example, 'Tortoise went to the pond. She caught 5 fish in her net. Two of them jumped back in the water. So she had 3 fish left.'

At the Races page 15

- Draw a horse of your own. Where is it and what is it doing?
- Find pictures of horses in magazines. Cut them out to make a collage.
- A horse's height is measured in hands. How many hands tall are you?
- Use construction equipment to make a field for some toy horses.

Beetles page 18

- Draw a family of beetles.
- Draw half a beetle. Get you friend to finish off the drawing. They must make sure it is symmetrical.
- How many legs does a beetle have? How many legs on 2 beetles? On 5 beetles?
- Make up a board game about beetles.
- Find out about different beetles. Which kind do you think is most interesting?
- Make a beetle out of clay or playdough. Weigh it when it is still wet and again when it is dry. What do you notice?

Clowns page 21

- Draw and colour a clown of your own.
- Paint your friend's face with face paints so he or she looks like a clown.
- Design and make a new bow tie for Clown 4.
- Design and make a hat for Clown 3.
- Make up a clown dance.
- Mime a funny act involving the clowns with a group of friends.

Crowns page 24

- Draw a crown to wear every day.
- Draw a crown to wear on a special occasion.
- Make a crown out of shiny paper and pretend jewels. Is it symmetrical?
- Find out what happens at a coronation.
- Listen to some coronation music.
- Everybody takes a turn to wear a crown, saying what they would do to help the world if they were a queen or king.
- Write a short poem about a Queen wearing her crown. It does not have to rhyme.

Dog Show page 27

- Draw a dog of your own ready for a dog show. What is its name?
- Draw the dogs with a thought bubble by each one. Write in the bubble what the dogs are thinking.
- Design and make a dog collar.
- Research different types of dog on the Internet. Which kind is your favourite?
- Read a story about a dog.
- Find some animal poems and discuss.

Dragons   page 30

- ❖ Draw a dragon of your own.
- ❖ Make a model dragon out of junk materials – egg boxes might be good.
- ❖ Make a collage of a dragon using different materials for the parts of its body.
- ❖ Think of words to describe a dragon. Write each word in a bubble and stick them all around your dragon picture.
- ❖ Read the story of St. George and the Dragon.
- ❖ Find out more about dragons from books or the Internet.
- ❖ Imagine you are one of the dragons, what do you think you might be saying to your friend. Try acting this out with a partner.

Fancy dress   page 33

- ❖ Draw someone in fancy dress.
- ❖ Choose a game you might play at a party. Write instructions for someone who doesn't know how to play it.
- ❖ Design an invitation for a fancy dress party.
- ❖ Make a mask to wear. Measure how far apart your eyes are so you get the eyeholes in the right place.

Fans   page 36

- ❖ Design a fan of your own.
- ❖ Describe your fan.
- ❖ Make a fan from lolly sticks and paper.
- ❖ Make a fan just by folding paper. What shape of paper do you think you need to start with? Try different shapes and see which works best.
- ❖ Think of words that rhyme with fan. How many can you find?

Patterns   page 39

- ❖ Use flat plastic shapes to make patterns.
- ❖ Design some wrapping paper using repeating patterns.
- ❖ Make a brooch or badge and decorate it with patterns.
- ❖ Make a mobile using cut-out flat shapes. Make a class display of animals made up from different shapes (triangle sheep, round cows ...).

Flowers   page 42

- ❖ Draw some crazy flowers. Choose your favourite colours to colour them.
- ❖ Look at a real flower very closely. Try to draw it just the way it is.
- ❖ Choose one of the vases in the picture but don't say which it is. Describe it. Can your friend work out which vase you chose?
- ❖ Paint large flowers for a class display. Make butterflies and bees to put on the flowers.
- ❖ Grow some nasturtiums or sweet peas.

Hair   page 45

- ❖ Pretend you have a hairdressing shop. Make a list of all the things you could do for your customers.
- ❖ Make up a price list for a hairdressing shop.
- ❖ Draw a child. How will you choose to do their hair?
- ❖ Find out about the class's favourite hairstyles and think about how to display the information.
- ❖ Design a special hairgrip or bobble.

Haunted House   page 48

- ❖ Paint or draw a haunted house.
- ❖ Make a haunted house from an old box. How will you decorate it?

8

❖ Read a story about monsters or ghosts to your friends.

Houses   page 51

❖ Read The Three Little Pigs.

❖ Choose a fairy tale character, such as Hansel and Gretel's witch, or Goldilocks' bears) and draw their house. Can your friend guess who lives there?

❖ As a class, collect ideas about materials you could use to build a real house.

❖ Find out about houses built from straw bales.

❖ Build a house out of construction material. Who lives in it?

Seals   page 54

❖ Look at books about seals and find out about where they live and what they eat.

❖ Draw a seal on a rock.

❖ Make a seal puppet out of felt. Make up a puppet show.

❖ Make a storyboard for a puppet show, using pictures.

Lizards   page 57

❖ Find out about real lizards. Where do they live and what do they eat?

❖ Draw a lizard.

❖ Make a lizard badge or brooch.

Cartoon Characters   page 60

❖ Invent your own cartoon character. Draw them and write about them. What do they do?

❖ Create a cartoon strip for your character.

❖ Find out about the cartoons that people in your class like watching. Is there a favourite?

Party   page 63

❖ Draw a picture of yourself at a party.

❖ Make sandwiches with healthy fillings.

❖ Decorate some paper plates.

❖ Explore different ways to cut sandwiches (eg halves, quarters).

❖ Design and make party hats.

❖ Make some jelly. Talk about how it changes when it's heated and then cooled.

Pictures   page 66

❖ Paint your own picture.

❖ Make a papier mâché frame for your picture and hang it on the wall.

❖ Give your picture an interesting name. Make a label for it with your name, the date you painted it, and its title.

❖ Decide how much to charge for the paintings people have done and make a price list.

❖ Go to an art gallery and look at paintings by different artists. Which do you like best?

Robots   page 69

❖ Draw a robot of your own.

❖ Use construction equipment to make a robot with moving arms and legs.

❖ Use batteries and a simple circuit to give your robot eyes which light up.

❖ Construct a giant robot out of boxes and other materials.

❖ Make up a special language for your robot. What might it say for 'yes' and 'no'?

❖ Make a robot which is a function machine. Feed it a number card and tell it what to do to the number (for example, 'add 5'). Ask your friend to help the robot choose the card with the right answer.

❖ Make up some robot music and dance to it, pretending you are a robot.

Knights page 72

- ❖ Draw Sir Robin's castle.
- ❖ Draw a knight of your own and make a class display. Is your knight in armour?
- ❖ Design two shields: one symmetrical and one not.
- ❖ Look at books on knights and castles.
- ❖ Draw a castle and label all the important features.
- ❖ Read the story of St George and the Dragon, or read about Sir Gawain.
- ❖ Have a medieval day where everyone dresses up.

Sea Creatures page 75

- ❖ Look at different types of fish in books or on the Internet. Draw one of them.
- ❖ Find out what fish eat.
- ❖ How big can fish be? How small?
- ❖ Make a bowl or plate from papier mâché and decorate it with a fish pattern.
- ❖ Make a fish mobile.
- ❖ Make fish out of clay and paint them.

Teeth page 78

- ❖ Draw someone with a lovely smile.
- ❖ Find out about teeth and how they are constructed.
- ❖ Find out about animals' teeth.
- ❖ Talk about dental hygiene. How often should you brush your teeth?
- ❖ Ella brushes her teeth twice a day. How often does she brush them in one week? And in a month?
- ❖ Invent a fabulous new toothbrush or toothpaste and do a quick television commercial to promote your new product!

Trees page 81

- ❖ Collect some leaves and try to find out what trees they come from.

- ❖ Experiment with leaf or bark rubbings.
- ❖ If the owl and cat could talk, what might they say to each other? Make speech bubbles and write what they say.
- ❖ Make a class achievement tree. Everyone cuts out a leaf and writes on it one thing they are good at.
- ❖ Make a target tree. Everyone cuts out a leaf and writes on it one thing they are going to try hard at this term.

Umbrellas page 84

- ❖ Look at an umbrella carefully and talk about how it is made.
- ❖ Test different fabrics and materials to find out which keep out the water.
- ❖ Paint a giant umbrella and decorate it.
- ❖ Brainstorm all the words you might use to describe a wet day: miserable, cold, blustery.
- ❖ Write a short story about an umbrella that blows away, where will it go?
- ❖ Write a poem about an umbrella.

Windows page 87

- ❖ Go on a walk round the school or neighbourhood. Take photographs of different kinds of windows. Back in school, find ways to sort the windows.
- ❖ Draw a window. How many panes does it have?
- ❖ Design some fabric for curtains.
- ❖ Make a window in a cardboard box. Decide whether it is divided up into panes. Make curtains for it from fabric scraps.
- ❖ Make 'stained glass' windows from black paper and tissue paper.

Under the Sea page 90

- ❖ Design and make a necklace from shells.
- ❖ Draw a mermaid.

- Sort a collection of shells. Present your findings as a block graph.
- Find out about the class's favourite sea creatures.
- Draw half a sea creature and ask a friend to draw the other half to make it symmetrical.

Famous Pictures   page 93

- Paint a strange picture of your own. Think up a name for it.
- Make a frame for your picture.
- Write a price label for your painting. How much will you charge?
- Look at some reproductions of famous paintings and decide which you like best.

Hobbies   page 96

- Make your own miniature climbing wall for a doll out of boxes and other materials.
- Design a swimming costume for Mona.
- Look at a variety of protective clothing people wear for roller blading and cycling. Discuss why it is important and what other hobbies and jobs may need protective clothing.
- Make a short presentation to the class about your favourite sport or hobby.
- Collect data about people's favourite hobbies in the class and make a chart to show this information. Write three questions about the chart for people to answer.

Scarlett's Birthday   page 99

- Choose three games you would like to play at a party. Find out which your class would most like to play, then play it.
- Draw a birthday cake.
- Make some cupcakes.
- Scarlett's mum made 12 rounds of sandwiches and cut them all in half. How many pieces were there then?
- Joe blows up 36 balloons but 14 of them burst. How many are left?
- Make a party hat shaped like a crown.
- Sing a birthday song.
- Make up a birthday song.

The Farmyard   page 102

- Draw Megan's farm. Make sure you show the different animals she keeps.
- Use wool to make a collage of a sheep or a sheepdog.
- Make a cake, or an omelette. How many eggs do you need?
- If Patrick collects 20 eggs every day for a week, how many eggs is that?
- Find out about chicken eggs and how they hatch.

The Unkind Parrot   page 105

- Create a class collage of a jungle with Percy in his tree.
- Draw a picture of Percy in the jungle. What is he doing?
- Research birds and creatures that live in a jungle.
- Find out about endangered jungle animals.
- With a friend, act out a conversation between the big bird and Percy. What do they say to each other?
- Act out the passage with some friends and then continue it to show what you think will happen next.

11

Animals

Dog

Tortoise

Seal

Rabbit

Yes or No

1. Tortoise has a net. _____

2. Seal has roller skates. _____

3. Rabbit has a ball. _____

4. Dog has a collar. _____

5. Rabbit has long ears. _____

Questions

Answer with a full sentence.

1. Who has a net?

2. Who has roller skates?

3. Who has long ears?

4. Who has a ball?

5. How many animals are there?

6. Who has not got legs?

Brilliant Activities for Reading Comprehension, Year 1

© Charlotte Makhlouf and Brilliant Publications

Extension work

1. Which of the animals in the picture do you like best? Why?

2. Which of the animals like going in water?

3. Think up names for the animals.

4. Name some animals that have whiskers.

5. What kind of animal would you like to have as a pet?

6. Make up a story about an animal.

At the Races

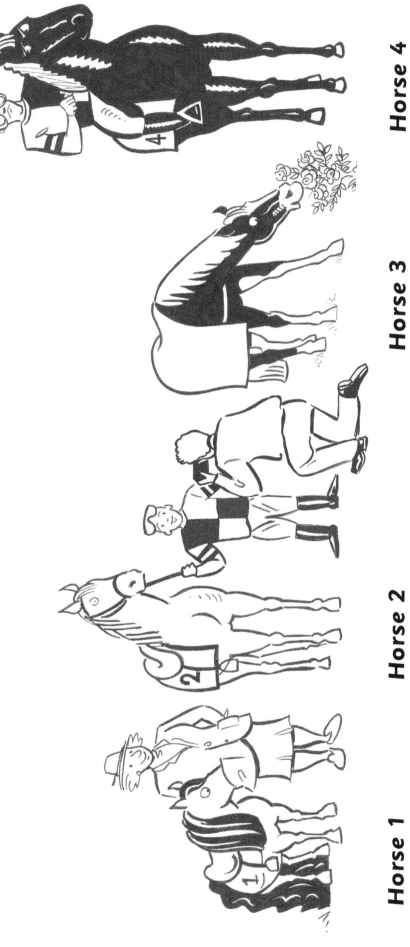

Horse 1

Horse 2

Horse 3

Horse 4

Yes or No

1. There are two horses. _____

2. Horse 4 has a rider. _____

3. Horse 4 is the smallest. _____

4. Horse 1 is the tallest. _____

5. There are three people. _____

6. Horse 2 is eating roses. _____

Questions

Answer with a full sentence.

1. How many horses can you see?

2. Which is the smallest horse?

3. How many riders can you see?

4. Which horse looks has the longest mane?

5. Does the rider of Horse 4 look happy or cross?

6. Which horse is wearing a blanket?

7. Which horse is eating flowers?

Extension work

1. Which is your favourite horse and why do you like it?

2. What do you think the Shetland pony, number 1, is doing?

3. Why do you think horse 3 is wearing a blanket?

4. Number 2 has just won a race. Choose a name for the horse.

5. Would you like to ride a horse? How do you think it would make you feel?

Beetles

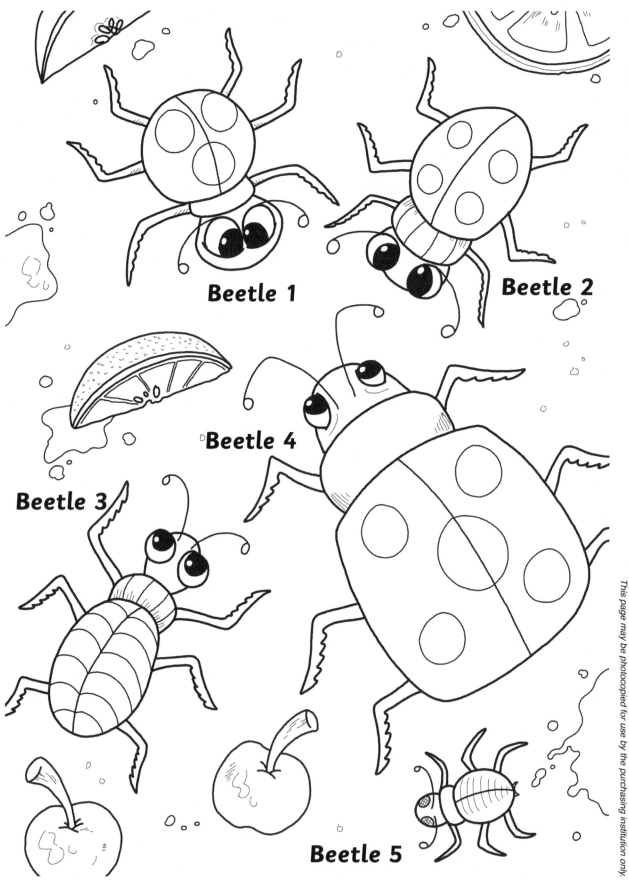

Beetle 1

Beetle 2

Beetle 4

Beetle 3

Beetle 5

18

Yes or No

1. Beetle 1 has spots. _____

2. Beetle 4 is biggest. _____

3. Beetle 2 has no spots. _____

4. Beetle 5 is small. _____

5. Beetle 3 has one spot. _____

Questions

Answer with a full sentence.

1. Which beetle is smallest?

2. Which is the biggest beetle?

3. Which beetles have no spots?

4. Which beetle has three spots?

5. Which beetles have six legs?

Extension work

1. Where might you find a beetle?

2. Lots of beetles can fly. Would you like to be able to fly?

3. Some beetles can swim. Do you like swimming?

4. Write a story about a beetle.

Clowns

Clown 4

Clown 3

Clown 2

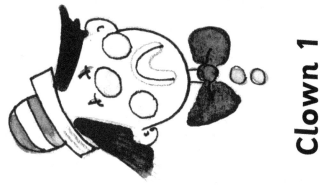

Clown 1

Yes or No

1. There are four clowns. _____

2. Clown 1 has a hat. _____

3. Clown 3 has a bow tie. _____

4. Clown 3 has a hat. _____

5. Clown 2 is happy. _____

6. Clown 1 is sad. _____

7. Clown 2 has a flower. _____

Questions

Answer with a full sentence.

1. How many clowns are there?

2. Which clown is sad?

3. Which clown has the biggest bow tie?

4. Which clown has the smallest bow tie?

5. What does Clown 4 have on her head?

6. Which clown does not have a bow tie?

Extension work

1. Which clown do you like best?

2. Where might you see a clown?

3. Imagine you are a clown. What would you wear?

4. Imagine you are a clown. What funny things would you do?

5. Write a story about a clown.

Crowns

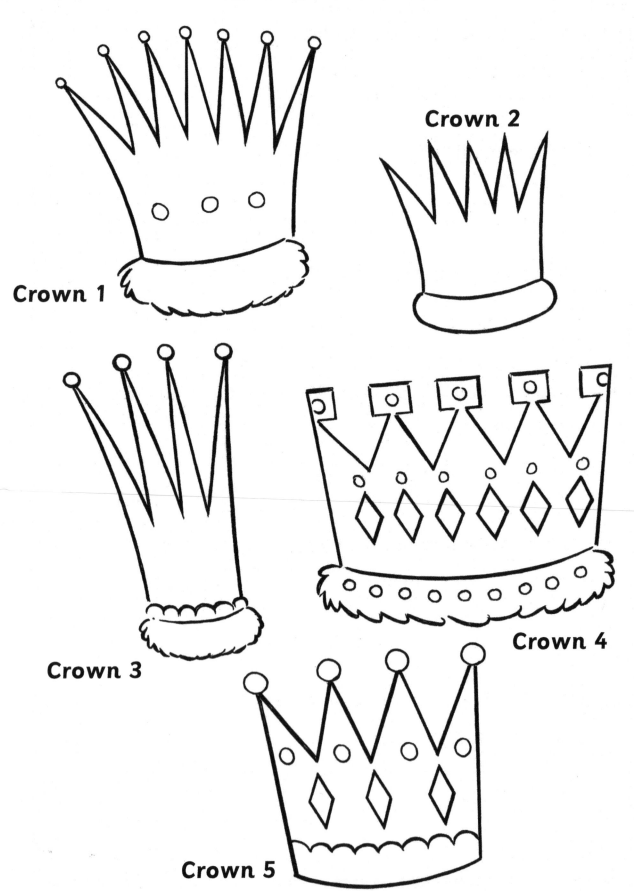

Crown 1

Crown 2

Crown 3

Crown 4

Crown 5

Brilliant Activities for Reading Comprehension, Year 1

Yes or No

1. Crown 1 is the smallest. _____

2. Crown 3 has square
   decorations. _____

3. Crown 2 is the largest. _____

4. There are five crowns. _____

Questions

Answer with a full sentence.

1. Which crown is the smallest?

2. Which crown is the widest?

3. How many crowns are there?

4. Which crowns have diamond decorations?

5. Which crown has no decoration?

Extension work

1. Which of these crowns would you choose for you and your friend to wear?

2. The crowns are in a museum. What else do you think you could see in a museum?

3. Imagine you are queen or king. Describe the crown you wear.

4. Write a story about a person who wears one of these crowns.

Brilliant Activities for Reading Comprehension, Year 1
© Charlotte Makhlouf and Brilliant Publications

Dog Show

Barney
2nd

Pip
5th

Fluffy
3rd

Bonzo
4th

Chow
1st

Yes or No

1. There are two dogs. _____
2. Fluffy has a bow. _____
3. Bonzo came third. _____
4. Chow came first. _____
5. Bonzo has a collar. _____

Questions

Answer with a full sentence.

1. Who is wearing a bow?

2. Which dog came 1st?

3. Which dog came 5th?

4. How many dogs are in the picture?

5. Which dog is the biggest?

6. Which dog is the smallest?

7. Which dog is wearing a collar with studs?

Extension work

1. If you were the judge, which dog would you choose to win 1st prize?

2. If you owned one of these dogs, which would you like it to be?

3. Think up some good names for dogs.

4. Write a story about one of the dogs.

Dragons

Dragon 1

Dragon 2

Brilliant Activities for Reading Comprehension, Year 1

Yes or No

1. There are two dragons.   _____

2. Both dragons have horns.   _____

3. Dragon 2 has not got a tail.   _____

4. Dragon 1 has smoke.   _____

Questions

Answer with a full sentence.

1. How many dragons are there?

2. Which dragon is wearing clothes?

3. Which dragon has smoke coming from its nose?

4. Has Dragon 1 got a tail?

5. What is Dragon 2 holding?

Extension work

1. The dragons are going to a party. Who else is at the party?

2. Do you think the dragons are looking forward to the party?

3. If you were a dragon how would you spend your time?

4. Write a story about a dragon.

Brilliant Activities for Reading Comprehension, Year 1
© Charlotte Makhlouf and Brilliant Publications

Fancy Dress

**Jo
Rabbit**

**Caz
Frog**

**Sam
Bear**

**Tug
Alien**

**Lin
Cat**

Yes or No

1. There are five people in fancy dress. _____

2. Caz is a frog. _____

3. Jo is a bear. _____

4. Lin is a cat. _____

5. Tug is a rabbit. _____

6. Sam is an alien. _____

7. Jo has big ears. _____

Questions

Answer with a full sentence.

1. How many people are in the picture?

2. Who is dressed as a bear?

3. Who is dressed as an alien?

4. How many people are dressed as animals?

5. Who is dressed as a rabbit?

Extension work

1. Suppose you were invited to a fancy dress party. What would you go as?

2. Suppose you want to dress as a tiger. What would you use for your costume?

3. Tug is sad. Think up a reason why.

Fans

Yes or No

1. Fan 3 has trees on it.   _____
2. Fan 1 has flowers on it.   _____
3. Fan 4 is broken.   _____
4. Fan 2 has flowers on it.   _____
5. Fan 3 is the biggest.   _____

Questions

Answer with a full sentence.

1. Which fan has flowers on it?

2. How many flowers does it have?

3. Which fan is broken?

4. How many trees are on fan 2?

5. Which fan is plain?

6. Which fan is the smallest?

Extension work

1. Which of the fans do you like best?

2. What do people use fans for?

3. What materials do you think fans might be made from?

Patterns

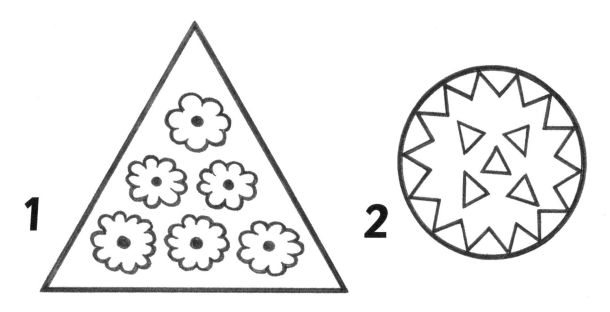

1

2

3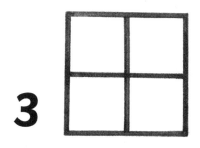

4

5

Brilliant Activities for Reading Comprehension, Year 1

© Charlotte Makhlouf and Brilliant Publications

Yes or No

1. There are three patterns. _____

2. Pattern 1 has flowers. _____

3. Pattern 3 is made of squares. _____

4. Pattern 4 has stripes. _____

5. Pattern 5 has spots. _____

Questions

Answer with a full sentence.

1. Which pattern has six sides?

2. Which pattern has three sides?

3. Which pattern has a zigzag in it?

4. Which pattern has six flowers in it?

5. Which pattern has triangles in it?

Extension work

1. Draw some patterns of your own and write down some questions about them for your friend to answer.

2. Write a list of words you can use to describe shapes and patterns.

Flowers

Brilliant Activities for Reading Comprehension, Year 1

© Charlotte Makhlouf and Brilliant Publications

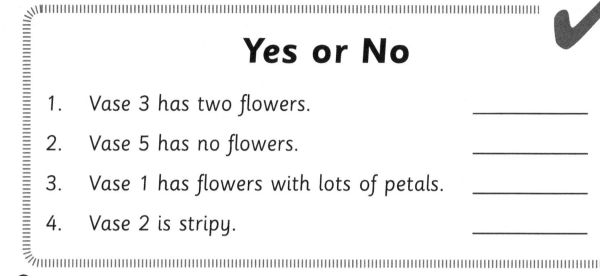

Yes or No

1. Vase 3 has two flowers. _____

2. Vase 5 has no flowers. _____

3. Vase 1 has flowers with lots of petals. _____

4. Vase 2 is stripy. _____

Questions

Answer with a full sentence.

1. How many flowers are there in vase 4?

2. Which vase has no flowers?

3. Which vase has spots?

4. Which vase has only one flower?

5. Which vase has very droopy flowers?

Extension work

1.   What names of flowers do you know?

2.   Write a story about a magic flower.

3.   Write a story about an elf that lives in a flower.

Hair

Shamlal

Thani

Flora

Harry

Em

Yes or No

1. There are three children. _____

2. Thani has long hair. _____

3. Harry has long hair. _____

4. Em has flowers in her hair. _____

5. Flora has a bow. _____

Questions

Answer with a full sentence.

1. How many children can you see?

2. Who has flowers in her hair?

3. Who has their hair on top of their head?

4. Who has the shortest hair?

Brilliant Activities for Reading Comprehension, Year 1
© Charlotte Makhlouf and Brilliant Publications

Extension work

1. What is your own hair like?

2. If your hair was different, how would you like it to be?

3. Who cuts your hair?

4. Do you like having your hair cut? Say why.

Haunted House

Brilliant Activities for Reading Comprehension, Year 1

© Charlotte Makhlouf and Brilliant Publications

Yes or No

1. There are no windows. _____

2. There are two trees. _____

3. There are four windows. _____

4. There is no door. _____

5. Four bats are flying. _____

6. The windows are broken. _____

Questions

Answer with a full sentence.

1. How many bats can you see?

2. What shape are the windows?

3. Are all the windows broken?

4. How many doors can you see?

5. Is there a chimney?

Extension work

1. What does *'haunted'* mean?

2. Write about the creatures that live in this house. Are they people? Ghosts? Monsters?

3. If you went inside the house what might you see?

4. Write a story about a haunted house.

Houses

Yes or No

1. House 1 has one window. _____

2. House 2 has a chimney. _____

3. House 3 is very big. _____

4. House 4 has two chimneys. _____

5. House 5 has one window. _____

Questions

Answer with a full sentence.

1. Which house has a very pointy roof?

2. Which house has a curved door?

3. Which is the smallest house?

4. Which house has most windows?

5. How many houses have chimneys?

Extension work

1. Which of these houses would you like to live in? Why?

2. Describe your own home. What do you like best about it?

3. Write a story about a house. Who lives in it?

4. Invent people to live in each house. What are their names?

Seals

Yes or No

1. Seal 1 is holding a fish.   _____

2. Seal 2 is juggling.   _____

3. Seal 3 is wearing a hat.   _____

4. Seal 4 has a net.   _____

5. Seal 5 has a teddy.   _____

Questions

Answer with a full sentence.

1. How many seals can you see?

2. Who has a net?

3. Which seal has a rocket?

4. Which seal is the smallest?

5. How many balls is Seal 2 juggling?

6. Which seal has a teddy?

Extension work

1. If you were a seal what would you like to do?

2. Invent two questions about the seals for a friend to answer.

3. Invent names for the seals.

4. Write a story about a seal that gets lost.

Lizards

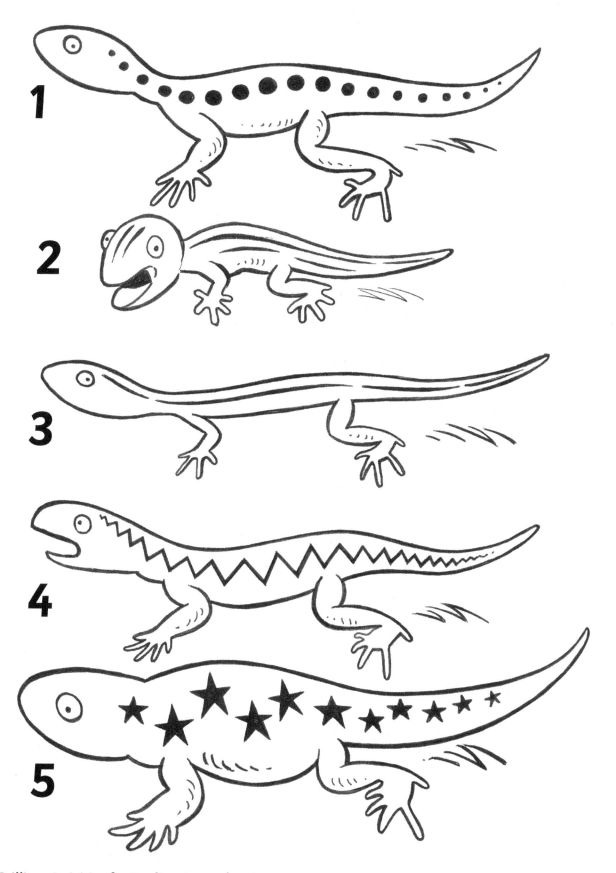

Brilliant Activities for Reading Comprehension, Year 1

Yes or No

1. Lizard 1 has spots. _____

2. Lizard 2 is the smallest. _____

3. Lizard 3 is the shortest. _____

4. Lizard 4 has zigzags. _____

5. Lizard 5 has spots. _____

Questions

Answer with a full sentence.

1. Which lizard has spots?

2. Which is the largest lizard?

3. Which lizard has stars on it?

4. Which lizard has zigzags?

5. How many lizards are there?

6. How many legs does a lizard have?

Extension work

1. Where do you think you might see a lizard?

2. Have you ever seen a lizard? If so, what was it like?

3. Think up some words to describe a lizard.

4. Do you like lizards? Say why or why not.

5. Which lizard do you think looks the scariest? Why?

Cartoon Characters

Smigwig

Trug

Glob

Plinkle

Brilliant Activities for Reading Comprehension, Year 1
© Charlotte Makhlouf and Brilliant Publications

Yes or No

1. Glob is a robot. _____

2. There are six characters. _____

3. Trug is a robot. _____

4. Plinkle is a mouse. _____

5. Smigwig is a carrot. _____

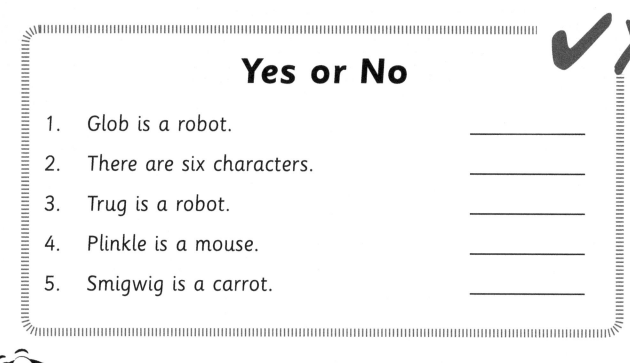

Questions

Answer with a full sentence.

1. Which character is a bird?

2. Who is holding an umbrella?

3. Who has wheels on their feet?

4. Who is holding a flower?

5. Which character looks sad?

6. Who has a very round belly?

Extension work

1. Make up a reason why Glob is sad.

2. Which character do you like best and why?

3. Plinkie has magic powers. What do you think they are?

4. Invent qualities for the four characters. What are they each like, and what do they do?

5. Make up a story about the four cartoon characters.

Party

Ben
Cherry
Cake

Raksha
Jelly

Pippa
Sandwiches

Sam
Popcorn

Rhys
Sausage
Rolls

Tina
Cupcake

Yes or No

1. There are two children. _____
2. There are three girls. _____
3. Ben has some cake. _____
4. Pippa is holding a drink. _____
5. Rhys is wearing a hat. _____
6. Tina is happy. _____
7. Sam has popcorn. _____
8. Tina has a cupcake. _____
9. Ben is wearing a dress. _____

Questions

Answer with a full sentence.

1. How many children can you see?

2. Who has jelly?

3. What does Ben have?

4. Who is eating a cupcake?

5. What is Pippa eating?

6. Who is wearing a shirt and tie?

7. Who is wearing a dress?

8. Who is crying?

Extension work

1. Do you think this is a fancy dress party? Explain your answer.

2. Suppose it's your party. What food would you like?

3. What games would you like to play at your party?

4. What else would you like to do at your party?

5. Write a story about a birthday party.

Pictures

1 **Lions**

2 **Moon**

3 **Shapes in my head**

4 **Light**

5 **Queen Tabitha**

Brilliant Activities for Reading Comprehension, Year 1

© Charlotte Makhlouf and Brilliant Publications

Yes or No

1. There are five pictures. _____

2. One picture has animals. _____

3. One picture shows the sun. _____

4. One picture shows the moon. _____

5. Two pictures show people. _____

Questions

Answer with a full sentence.

1. How many pictures are there altogether?

2. In which picture can you see hills?

3. Who is the woman in picture 5?

4. How is the woman in picture 5 special?

5. Which picture is round?

6. What is picture 3 called?

Extension work

1. Which is your favourite picture and why?

2. Can you think of another title for the picture called Light?

3. Do you think Lions is a good title for picture 1? Why?

4. Imagine you are an artist. Which do you like doing best: painting, drawing, printing or modelling?

5. Write a story about the lions or about Queen Tabitha.

Robots

Tigwig

Zizz

Foz

Zob

Yes or No

1. There are five robots. _____

2. One robot has numbers on its tummy. _____

3. All the robots have wheels. _____

4. Zob has one leg. _____

5. Tigwig has three legs. _____

6. Zizz has four arms _____

Questions

Answer with a full sentence.

1. How many robots are there?

2. Which robots have wheels?

3. Which robot has triangles for feet?

4. Which robot is the thinnest?

5. Which robot has spikes?

6. How many eyes does Zizz have?

7. How many arms does Foz have?

Extension work

1. Say which robot you like best and why you like it.

2. The robots live with people and help by doing jobs for them. Make up jobs for each of the robots.

3. Invent a reason why Zizz has numbers on its tummy.

4. Write a story about a robot which goes wrong and causes all sorts of trouble.

Knights

Sir Brian of Bracon lives in Misery Manor

Lord Smig of Woogs lives in Pobbleham

Sir Gluff of Gloop lives in Spain

Sir Robin of Pluggle lives in Castle Glog

Sir Tom of Dugwick lives in Castle Twig

Brilliant Activities for Reading Comprehension, Year 1

Yes or No

1. Sir Robin lives in Castle Glog. _____

2. Sir Tom lives in Castle Tree. _____

3. Lord Smig lives in Pobbleham. _____

4. Sir Gluff lives in Spain. _____

5. Sir Brian lives in Happy House. _____

Questions

Answer with a full sentence.

1. How many knights can you see?

2. Which knight has hearts on his tabard?

3. Who has diamonds on his tabard?

4. Which knight has a letter on his tabard?

5. Where does Sir Gluff live?

6. Who lives in Misery Manor?

Extension work

1. Which is your favourite knight? Why?

2. What do you think the B stands for on the Misery Manor knight's tabard?

3. Choose which knight you think is the most important. Why do you think this?

4. Choose a knight and invent a family for him. Who does he live with?

5. Write a story about a knight going on a quest to fight a dragon.

Brilliant Activities for Reading Comprehension, Year 1
© Charlotte Makhlouf and Brilliant Publications

Sea Creatures

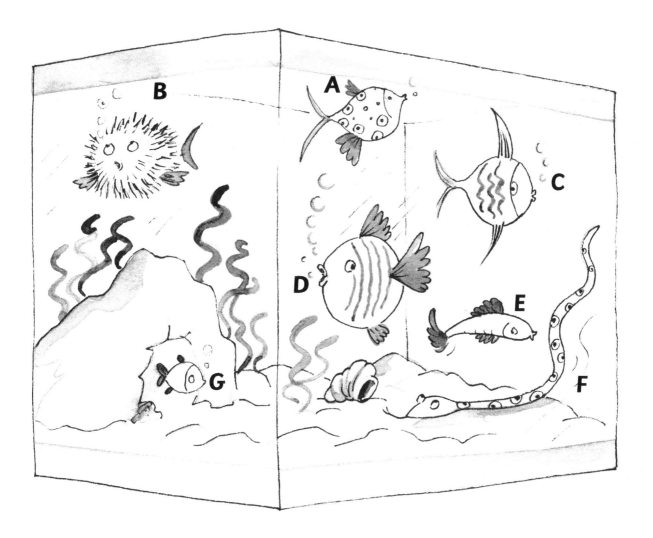

A   **Jarna the Jewel Fish**
B   **Spike the Sea Urchin**
C   **Sammy the Angel Fish**
D   **Puff the Bloater Fish**
E   **Lacey the Flutter Fish**
F   **Cyril the Sea Snake**
G   **Bob**

Yes or No

1. There are two fish. _____
2. Bob is the biggest. _____
3. Cyril is a sea snake. _____
4. Sammy has stripes. _____
5. Jarna is a jewel fish. _____

Questions

Answer with a full sentence.

1. Who has spots?

2. How many sea snakes can you see?

3. Who is the smallest fish?

4. What kind of fish is Lacey?

5. What is the bloater fish called?

Extension work

1. Which fish do you like best?

2. If you were a fish what would you like to do?

3. Suppose you were in the sea and you saw a sea snake. What would you do?

4. Write a story about a fish that learns to walk on dry land.

Teeth

Hayley

Rashid

Jack

Ella

Brilliant Activities for Reading Comprehension, Year 1

Yes or No

1. There are five people. _____

2. Rashid has gaps in his teeth. _____

3. Jack is a baby. _____

4. Rashid is a grown-up. _____

5. Ella has no teeth. _____

Questions

Answer with a full sentence.

1. How many people can you see?

2. Who do you think has the fewest teeth?

3. Who is wearing a tie?

4. Who has earrings?

5. Who is the youngest?

6. What does Hayley have round her neck?

Extension work

1. Write a story about a day in the life of a tooth fairy.

2. What do you think Jack is crying about?

3. Why do you think people have braces on their teeth?

4. Ask a friend to count your teeth. How many do you have?

Brilliant Activities for Reading Comprehension, Year 1
© Charlotte Makhlouf and Brilliant Publications

Trees

Yes or No

1. Tree 2 has four apples. _____

2. There is an owl in Tree 1. _____

3. There is a girl by Tree 1. _____

4. Tree 3 is small. _____

5. Tree 4 is tall. _____

Questions

Answer with a full sentence.

1. Which tree has a funny looking cat in it?

2. Which is the apple tree?

3. Where is the spider?

4. Where is the owl?

5. Who is under Tree 1?

6. Which tree is the smallest?

Extension work

1. What animals might you see in a tree?

2. What animals would you not expect to see in a tree?

3. Name some fruits that grow on trees.

4. Write a story about a cat that climbs a tree and can't get down.

5. Write a story about an owl that lives in a tree.

Umbrellas

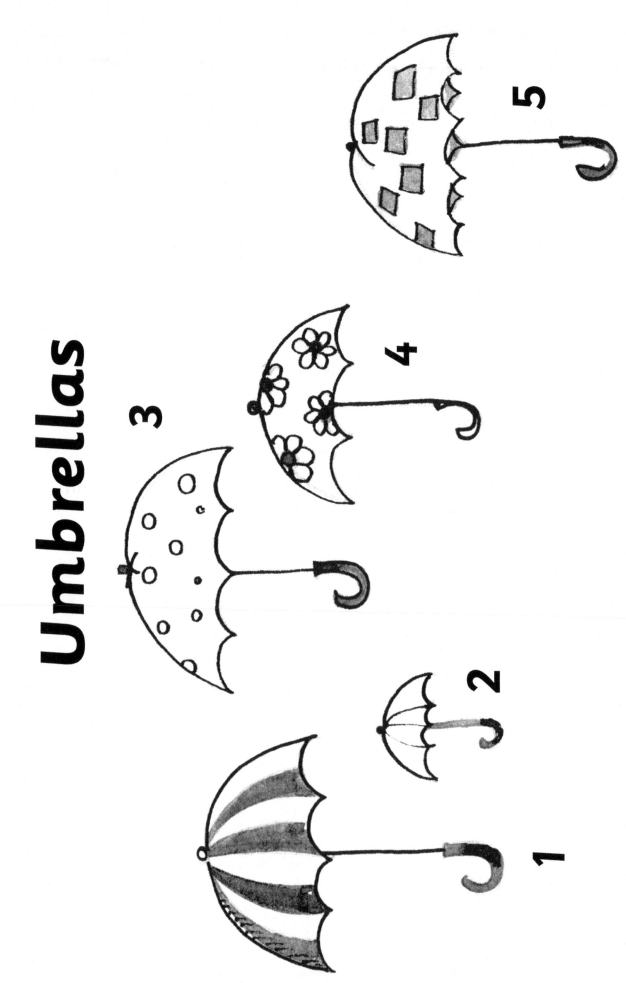

Brilliant Activities for Reading Comprehension, Year 1

Yes or No

1. There are four umbrellas. _____

2. There are flowers on
   Umbrella 4. _____

3. Umbrella 2 is the biggest. _____

4. Umbrella 5 has squares on it. _____

Questions

Answer with a full sentence.

1. Which umbrella has spots?

2. Which umbrella has stripes?

3. How many umbrellas are there?

4. Which is the smallest umbrella?

5. How many flowers are there on Umbrella 4?

6. Which umbrella has squares?

Extension work

1. When do people use umbrellas?

2. What do you wear to keep dry when it rains?

3. Write a story about an umbrella on a wet, windy day.

4. Write a story about a flood.

Brilliant Activities for Reading Comprehension, Year 1
© Charlotte Makhlouf and Brilliant Publications

Windows

Yes or No

1. There are five windows. _____

2. Window 1 has curtains. _____

3. Window 2 has curtains. _____

4. There are flowers in Window 6. _____

5. There is a cat in Window 3. _____

Questions

Answer with a full sentence.

1. How many windows are there?

2. Which windows have curtains?

3. Which window is broken?

4. Which window has shutters?

5. In which window is the cat?

6. Where can you see a person?

Brilliant Activities for Reading Comprehension, Year 1

Extension work

1. Why do people use curtains or shutters?

2. Choose one of the windows and describe the house it belongs to.

3. How do you think Window 3 got broken?

4. Choose a real window to look through. What can you see?

5. Write a story about a magic window. What do people see when they look through it?

Under the Sea

Under the sea the whales sing to each other.

Fish swim in and out of coral.

Mermaids comb their hair.

They make necklaces out of shells.

Crabs hide in their shells.

Brilliant Activities for Reading Comprehension, Year 1
© Charlotte Makhlouf and Brilliant Publications

Questions

Answer the questions with a full sentence.

1. What do the whales do under the sea?

2. What do the fish do?

3. Who likes to comb their hair?

4. What do mermaids make from shells?

5. Where do the crabs hide?

Extension work

1. What would you do if you could go under the sea?

2. List some creatures which live under the sea.

3. What sea creature would you like to meet? Why?

4. What sea creature would you not like to meet? Why?

5. Write about a mermaid. What is she called? Where does she live? What does she do?

Brilliant Activities for Reading Comprehension, Year 1
© Charlotte Makhlouf and Brilliant Publications

Famous Pictures

£500

Bumbleblot   by Irma Muckup

Painted in 1990 while the artist was visiting the town of Bughole. Muckup is known to love mountains and mice.

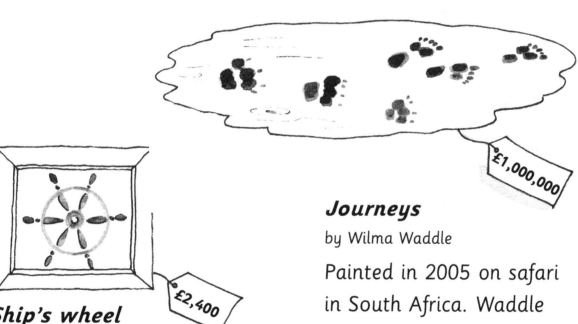

£1,000,000

Journeys

by Wilma Waddle

Painted in 2005 on safari in South Africa. Waddle has been painting since she was 3 years old. Animals are a favourite topic for her paintings.

£2,400

Ship's wheel

by Aron Biggs

Painted in 2010 in Paris. Aron Biggs lives on a boat and loves the sea.

Questions

Answer with a full sentence.

1. Who painted *Ship's wheel*?

2. Who painted *Bumbleblot*?

3. When was *Journeys* painted?

4. Where did Aron Biggs paint his picture?

5. Where did Wilma Waddle paint her picture?

6. What does Aron Biggs love?

7. Who likes doing paintings about animals?

Brilliant Activities for Reading Comprehension, Year 1
© Charlotte Makhlouf and Brilliant Publications

Extension work

1. If you could buy one of these pictures, which would you choose and why?

2. How long ago was *Ship's wheel* painted?

3. Which of the three paintings is cheapest? Which is most expensive?

4. Choose one of the artists. Write a piece about their life for a newspaper.

5. If you were a famous artist, what would you paint?

Hobbies

Gerry likes roller blading.

He has been roller blading for two years.

Gerry has fallen over eight times.

He wears a helmet, gloves and knee pads.

Reena does karate.

She has just got her black belt.

Reena is very good at karate.

She has won five competitions.

Dusan likes rock climbing.

He goes climbing at his sports centre.

Dusan likes climbing the high wall.

He would like to climb Mount Everest.

Mona likes swimming.

She swims like a fish.

She is very good at backstroke.

Mona wears her lucky red swimsuit.

Questions

Answer with a full sentence.

1. What does Dusan like doing?

2. What is Reena's hobby?

3. Who has a lucky red swimsuit?

4. What does Dusan hope to climb?

5. How many competitions has Reena won?

6. How many times has Gerry fallen?

Extension work

1. What happens at a sports centre?

2. If Mona '*swims like a fish*' what do you think this means?

3. Why do you think Gerry wears a helmet, gloves and knee pads?

4. What is your favourite hobby and why?

5. Which one of the hobbies above would you most like to try and why?

Brilliant Activities for Reading Comprehension, Year 1

© Charlotte Makhlouf and Brilliant Publications

Scarlett's Birthday

Scarlett is having a birthday party for her friends. They are having three different kinds of jelly, a huge birthday cake shaped like a ladybird, and a plate piled high with sandwiches.

On a table there are presents waiting for Scarlett. Her mum and auntie have already given her a bike.

Mr Twizzle the magician has come to the party. He has brought his rabbit, Sammy, which pops out of a black hat. Sammy has soft white fur and likes to be stroked.

Mr Twizzle makes balloon animals for all the children. He makes Scarlett an elephant out of green balloons and he makes Joe a dog out of red balloons.

At the end of the party, Scarlett gives out party bags to all her friends.

Questions

Answer with a full sentence.

1. Who is having the birthday party?

2. What present did Scarlett get from her mum and auntie?

3. Who is Mr Twizzle?

4. What has Mr Twizzle brought with him?

5. What type of cake is Scarlett having?

6. What does Mr Twizzle make for Scarlett?

7. How many types of jelly will there be?

8. What can you find on the table?

Brilliant Activities for Reading Comprehension, Year 1

© Charlotte Makhlouf and Brilliant Publications

Extension work

1. What flavours of jelly would you have if it was your party?

2. What do you think might be in the party bags?

3. If you had a party, what type of cake would you like?

4. What presents do you think Scarlett might be hoping for?

5. Suppose Mr Twizzle says he will make something out of balloons for you. What would you like?

The Farmyard

Megan is a farmer. She has a sheepdog called Woody who enjoys rounding up the sheep.

Megan has twenty pigs who like rolling in their muddy field.

Every morning, Patrick, Megan's son, feeds the chickens and collects the eggs. The chickens live in a big hut and they have a green field to scratch around in.

The farm cat likes to sleep on the wall in the warm sun.

Brilliant Activities for Reading Comprehension, Year 1

Questions

Answer with a full sentence.

1. What job does Megan do?

2. Who is Woody?

3. What does Woody enjoy doing?

4. How many pigs does Megan have?

5. What does Patrick do every morning?

6. Who likes sleeping on a wall?

7. What do the pigs enjoy doing?

Extension work

1. At night, what animal is a danger to the chickens?

2. At night-time, where do you think the chickens go to keep safe?

3. What do you think Megan and Patrick do with the eggs?

4. If you had a farm, what animals would you like to keep?

5. Why does Woody round up the sheep?

6. Write a story about the farm.

Brilliant Activities for Reading Comprehension, Year 1
© Charlotte Makhlouf and Brilliant Publications

The Unkind Parrot

Percy was not a kind parrot. He lived in a beautiful tree in the middle of the jungle. The tree was filled with lovely berries which Percy liked to eat.

'Go away!' he'd shout at the other birds if they tried to eat the berries. 'This is my tree!'

One day while Percy was asleep on the top branch, a large bird flew down beside him and woke him up.

'Go away!' shouted Percy. 'This is my tree and I'm sleeping here!'

'Please don't shout,' said the large bird. 'I've got a headache.' Percy looked shocked. No-one had spoken back to him before.

Questions

Answer with a full sentence.

1. What kind of bird is Percy?

2. Where does Percy live?

3. What is the tree filled with?

4. Why does Percy shout at the other birds?

5. The large bird asks Percy to stop shouting. Why?

6. Why is Percy shocked by the large bird?

Extension work

1. What do you think you would say to Percy if he shouted at you?

2. What does it mean that no-one had '*spoken back*' to Percy?

3. Do you think Percy is unkind?

4. Describe the jungle where Percy lives.

5. Write a list of words the jungle birds might use to describe Percy.

6. Write about what happens next to Percy.

7. Write a story about a person or animal that is no good at sharing. Do they learn to share in the end?

Answers

Animals *(page 12)*
Yes or No
1. Yes
2. No
3. No
4. Yes
5. Yes

Questions
1. Tortoise has a net.
2. Dog has roller skates.
3. Rabbit has long ears.
4. Seal has a ball.
5. There are four animals. (accept four in words and not in a number)
6. Seal has not got legs.

Extension work
(All the questions require personal response so the answers will vary.)

At the Races *(page 15)*
Yes or No
1. No
2. Yes
3. No
4. No
5. No
6. No

Questions
1. I can see four horses.
2. Horse 1 is the smallest horse.
3. I can see two riders.
4. Horse 1 has the longest mane.
5. The rider of Horse 4 looks cross.
6. Horse 3 is wearing a blanket.
7. Horse 3 is eating flowers.

Extension work
(All the questions require personal response so the answers will vary.)

Beetles *(page 18)*
Yes or No
1. Yes
2. Yes
3. No
4. Yes
5. No

Questions
1. Beetle 5 is the smallest.
2. Beetle 4 is the biggest.
3. Beetles 3 and 5 have no spots.
4. Beetle 1 has three spots.
5. All the beetles have six legs.

Extension work
(All the questions require personal response so the answers will vary.)

Clowns *(page 21)*
Yes or No
1. Yes
2. Yes
3. Yes
4. No
5. Yes
6. Yes
7. Yes

Questions
1. There are four clowns.
2. Clown 1 is sad.
3. Clown 4 has the biggest bow tie.
4. Clown 1 has the smallest bow tie.
5. Clown 4 has a carrot on her head.
6. Clown 2 does not have a bow tie.

Extension work
(All the questions require personal response so the

Crowns *(page 24)*
Yes or No
1. No
2. No
3. No
4. Yes

Questions
1. Crown 2 is the smallest.
2. Crown 4 is the widest.
3. There are five crowns.
4. Crowns 4 and 5 have diamond decorations OR Crown 4 and Crown 5 have diamond decorations.
5. Crown 2 has no decorations.

Extension work
All the questions require personal response so the answers will vary.

Dog Show *(page 27)*
Yes or No
1. No
2. Yes
3. No
4. Yes
5. Yes

Questions
1. Fluffy has a bow.
2. Chow came first.
3. Pip came fifth.
4. Five dogs are in the picture.
5. Barney is the biggest.
6. Chow is the smallest.
7. Bonzo is wearing a collar with studs.

Extension work
(All the questions require personal response so the answers will vary.)

Brilliant Activities for Reading Comprehension, Year 1

Dragons (page 30)
Yes or No
1. Yes
2. Yes
3. No
4. Yes

Questions
1. There are two dragons.
2. Dragon 2 is wearing clothes.
3. Dragon 1 has smoke coming from his nose.
4. Yes, Dragon 1 has a tail.
5. Dragon 2 is holding some balloons.

Extension work
(All the questions require personal response so the answers will vary.)

Fancy Dress (page 33)
Yes or No
1. Yes
2. Yes
3. No
4. Yes
5. No
6. No
7. Yes

Questions
1. There are five people in the picture.
2. Sam is dressed as a bear.
3. Tug is dressed as an alien.
4. Four people are dressed as animals.
5. Jo is dressed as a rabbit.

Extension work
(All the questions require personal response so the answers will vary.)

Fans (page 36)
Yes or No
1. No
2. No
3. Yes
4. No
5. Yes

Questions
1. Fan 3 has flowers on it.
2. It has six flowers.
3. Fan 4 is broken.
4. There are two trees on fan 2.
5. Fan 4 is plain.
6. Fan 2 is the smallest.

Extension work
(All the questions require personal response so the answers will vary.)

Patterns (page 39)
Yes or No
1. No
2. Yes
3. Yes
4. Yes
5. Yes

Questions
1. Pattern 5 has six sides.
2. Pattern 1 has three sides.
3. Pattern 2 has a zigzag in it.
4. Pattern 1 has six flowers in it.
5. Pattern 2 has triangles on it.

Extension work
(All the questions require personal response so the answers will vary.)

Flowers (page 42)
Yes or No
1. No
2. Yes
3. Yes
4. No

Questions
1. Vase 4 has four flowers.
2. Vase 5 has no flowers.
3. Vase 3 has spots.
4. Vase 3 has only one flower.
5. Vase 4 has very droopy flowers.

Extension work
(All the questions require personal response so the answers will vary.)

Hair (page 45)
Yes or No
1. No
2. Yes
3. No
4. Yes
5. Yes

Questions
1. I can see five children.
2. Em has flowers in her hair.
3. Shamlal has his hair on top of his head.
4. Harry has the shortest hair.

Extension work
(All the questions require personal response so the answers will vary.)

Haunted House (page 48)
Yes or No
1. No
2. No
3. Yes
4. No
5. Yes
6. Yes

Questions
1. I can see four bats.
2. Some of the windows are square and some are rounded at the top.
3. All the windows are broken.
4. I can see two doors.
5. There is one chimney.

Extension work
(All the questions require personal response so the answers will vary.)

Houses (page 51)
Yes or No
1. No
2. Yes
3. No
4. No
5. Yes

Questions
1. House 5 has a very pointy roof.
2. House 2 has a curved door.
3. House 3 is the smallest house.
4. House 4 has the most windows.
5. Four houses have chimneys.

Extension work
(All the questions require personal response so the answers will vary.)

Seals (page 54)
Yes or No
1. Yes
2. Yes
3. No
4. No
5. Yes

Questions
1. I can see five seals.
2. Seal 3 has a net.
3. Seal 4 has a rocket.
4. Seal 2 is the smallest.
5. Seal 2 is juggling seven balls.
6. Seal 5 has a teddy.

Extension work
(All the questions require personal response so the answers will vary.)

Lizards (page 57)
Yes or No
1. Yes
2. Yes
3. No
4. Yes

5. No

Questions
1. Lizard 1 has spots.
2. Lizard 5 is the longest lizard.
3. Lizard 5 has stars on it.
4. Lizard 4 has zigzags on it.
5. There are five lizards.
6. Lizards have four legs.

Extension work
(All the questions require personal response so the answers will vary.)

Cartoon Characters (page 60)
Yes or No
1. Yes
2. No
3. Yes
4. Yes
5. No

Questions
1. Smigwig is a bird.
2. Glob is holding an umbrella.
3. No-one has wheels on their feet.
4. Smigwig is holding a flower.
5. Glob looks sad.
6. Trug has a very round belly.

Extension work
(All the questions require personal response so the answers will vary.)

Party (page 63)
Yes or No
1. No
2. Yes
3. Yes
4. No
5. No
6. Yes
7. Yes
8. Yes
9. No

Questions
1. I can see six children.
2. Raksha has jelly.
3. Ben has cherry cake.
4. Tina is eating a cupcake.
5. Pippa is eating sandwiches.
6. Sam is wearing a shirt and tie.
7. Raksha and Tina are wearing a dress.
8. Rhys is crying.

Extension work
(All the questions require personal response so the answers will vary.)

Pictures (page 66)
Yes or No
1. Yes
2. Yes
3. Yes
4. Yes
5. No

Questions
1. There are five pictures altogether.
2. I can see hills in picture 1.
3. The woman in picture 5 is Queen Tabitha.
4. She is special because she is a queen.
5. Picture 2 is round.
6. Picture 3 is called shapes in my head.

Extension work
(All the questions require personal response so the answers will vary.)

Robots (page 69)
Yes or No
1. No
2. Yes
3. No
4. Yes
5. No
6. No

Questions
1. There are four robots.
2. Zizz and Zob have wheels.
3. Foz has triangles for feet.
4. Foz is the thinnest robot.
5. Tigwig has spikes. OR Tigwig has spikes on his shoulders.
6. Zizz has one eye.
7. Foz has three arms.

Extension work
(All the questions require personal response so the answers will vary.)

Knights *(page 72)*
Yes or No
1. Yes
2. No
3. Yes
4. Yes
5. No

Questions
1. I can see five knights.
2. Lord Smig has hearts on his tabard.
3. Sir Gluff has diamonds on his tabard.
4. Sir Brian has a letter on his tabard.
5. Sir Gluff lives in Spain.
6. Sir Brian of Bracon lives in Misery Manor.

Extension work
(All the questions require personal response so the answers will vary.)

Sea Creatures *(page 75)*
Yes or No
1. No
2. No
3. Yes
4. Yes
5. Yes

Questions
1. Jarna the Jewel Fish and Cyril the Sea Snake have

spots.
2. I can see one sea snake.
3. The smallest fish is Bob.
4. Lacey is a flutter fish.
5. The bloater fish is called Puff.

Extension work
(All the questions require personal response so the answers will vary.)

Teeth *(page 78)*
Yes or No
1. No
2. Yes
3. Yes
4. No
5. No

Questions
1. I can see four people.
2. I think that Jack has the fewest teeth.
3. Rashid is wearing a tie.
4. Ella has earrings.
5. Jack is the youngest.
6. Hayley has a scarf around her neck.

Extension work
(All the questions require personal response so the answers will vary.)

Trees *(page 81)*
Yes or No
1. Yes
2. No
3. Yes
4. Yes
5. Yes

Questions
1. Tree 4 has a funny looking cat in it.
2. Tree 2 is the apple tree.
3. The spider is in tree 1.
4. The owl is in tree 5.
5. A girl is under tree 1.
6. Tree 3 is the smallest.

Extension work
(All the questions require personal response so the answers will vary.)

Umbrellas *(page 84)*
Yes or No
1. No
2. Yes
3. No
4. Yes

Questions
1. Umbrella 3 has spots.
2. Umbrella 1 has stripes.
3. There are five umbrellas
4. Umbrella 2 is the smallest umbrella.
5. There are four flowers on Umbrella 4.
6. Umbrella 5 has squares.

Extension work
(All the questions require personal response so the answers will vary.)

Windows *(page 87)*
Yes or No
1. No
2. No
3. Yes
4. Yes
5. No

Questions
1. There are six windows.
2. Windows 2 and 5 have curtains.
3. Window 3 is broken.
4. Window 4 has shutters.
5. The cat is in window 1.
6. I can see a person in window 5.

Extension work
(All the questions require personal response so the answers will vary.)

Under the Sea (page 90)
Questions
1. The whales sing to each other under the sea.
2. The fish swim in and out of coral.
3. The mermaids like to comb their hair.
4. The mermaids make necklaces out of shells.
5. The crabs hide in their shells.

Extension work
(All the questions require personal response so the answers will vary.)

Famous Pictures (page 93)
Questions
1. Ship's Wheel was painted by Aron Biggs.
2. Bumbleblot was painted by Irma Muckup.
3. Journeys was painted in 2005.
4. Aron Biggs painted his picture in Paris.
5. Wilma Waddle painted her picture on safari in South Africa.
6. Aron Biggs loves the sea.
7. Wilma Waddle loves painting pictures about animals.

Extension work
1. (A personal response is required so answers will vary.)
2. (This answer will vary depending on which year the passage is read.)
3. The cheapest painting is the Bumbleblot at £500. The most expensive is Journeys at £1 000 000.
4-5. (Require an imaginative and personal response.)

Hobbies (page 96)
Questions
1. Dusan likes rock climbing.
2. Reena's hobby is karate.
3. Mona has a lucky red swimsuit.
4. Dusan hopes to climb Mount Everest.
5. Reena has won five competitions.
6. Gerry has fallen over eight times!

Extension work
1. (Answers will vary for this question but there should be some mention of the different things that can be done at a sports centre.)
2. 'Swims like a fish' means that Mona is very happy and comfortable in the water and she swims so well she can be likened to a fish which also swims very well.
3. I think Gerry wears a helmet, knee pads and gloves so that he can protect himself if he falls over.
4. My favourite hobby is … because … .
5. I would most like to try … because … .

Scarlett's Birthday (page 99)
Questions
1. Scarlett is having the birthday party.
2. Scarlett got a bike from her mum and her auntie.
3. Mr Twizzle is the magician.
4. Mr Twizzle has brought his rabbit Sammy with him.
5. Scarlett is having a ladybird shaped cake.
6. Mr Twizzle makes an elephant for Scarlett out of green balloons.
7. There will be three different kinds of jelly.

8. You can find the presents on the table.

Extension work
(All the questions require personal response so the answers will vary.)

The Farmyard (page 102)
Questions
1. Megan is a farmer.
2. Woody is the sheepdog.
3. Woody enjoys rounding up the sheep.
4. Megan has twenty pigs.
5. Every morning Patrick feeds the chickens and collects the eggs.
6. The farm cat likes to sleep on the wall.
7. The pigs enjoy rolling about in their muddy field.

Extension work
1. At night the fox is a danger to the chickens.
2. The chickens go into their special hut (chicken coop) to keep safe.
3. I think Megan and Patrick eat the eggs. OR I think Megan and Patrick have scrambled eggs. OR I think Megan and Patrick sell their eggs at market. (accept sensible variations)
4. If I had a farm I would keep … .
5. Woody rounds up the sheep because he is a sheepdog and that is what his instinct tells him to do. (accept sensible variations)
6. (Personal creative response required.)

The Unkind Parrot (page 105)
Questions
1. Percy is a parrot.
2. Percy lives in a tree in the middle of the jungle.
3. The tree is filled with lovely

Brilliant Activities for Reading Comprehension, Year 1
© Charlotte Makhlouf and Brilliant Publications

berries.

4. Percy shouts at the other birds so that they do not eat his berries.

5. The large bird asks him to stop shouting because he has a headache.

6. Percy is shocked because no-one has spoken back to him before.

Extension work
(All the questions require personal response so the answers will vary.)

Lightning Source UK Ltd.
Milton Keynes UK
UKOW04f0145271116

288595UK00002B/15/P

9 780857 474827